THE BEAUTYBOX

ADRIANA LUNA CARLOS
Editor-In-Chief, Designer
and Co-Founder

HANNA OLIVAS
Managing Editor &
Co-Founder

NICOLE CURTIS
Director of the SRS
Magazine Division

ADVERTISING OPPORTUNITIES

Info@SheRisesStudios.com

THE BEAUTY BOX MAGAZINE
MAY 2025

SHE RISES
STUDIOS

CONTACT US

SheRisesStudios@gmail.com

WWW.SHERISESSTUDIOS.COM

LETTER FROM THE **EDITORS**

Dear Reader,

Welcome to the May 2025 edition of The Beauty Box Magazine — where beauty meets power, and confidence blooms in full color. As nature comes alive again, so do we. This season of renewal inspired us to curate a vibrant and empowering collection of beauty, fashion, and wellness stories designed to help you refresh your routine and radiate confidence from the inside out.

In this edition, themed Radiate Confidence: Beauty, Wellness & Style in Full Bloom, we explore how self-expression through style, skincare, and self-care can become a catalyst for personal empowerment. Whether it's a bold lipstick, a powerful morning ritual, or a style that speaks to your soul, we believe confidence begins with honoring who you are in every facet of your life.

We are honored to feature Lovely LaGuerre on our front cover — a visionary leader, author, and founder of Pure Heavenly Hair and Beauty Boutique. Her story is one of resilience, faith, and divine confidence, reminding us all of the power in embracing our identity and showing up boldly in our purpose.

As you flip through these pages, we hope you feel inspired to elevate your beauty, embrace your power, and step fully into your light. This month, let your style speak volumes, let your rituals ground you, and let your confidence bloom.

Warm regards,

Adriana Luna Carlos, Hanna Olivas and Nicole Curtis
Editors of The Beauty Box Magazine

SHE WINS GLOBAL SUMMIT 2025

This is more than an event—it's a movement!

Join 500+ unstoppable women for two days of powerful keynotes, celebrity fireside chats, business growth strategies, and high-level networking. Elevate your career, expand your influence, and connect with industry leaders shaping the future!

Want To Take The Stage!

We're inviting dynamic speakers to share expertise on finance, leadership, branding, health, tech, and more! Elevate your voice, gain global exposure on FENIX TV, and unlock Exclusive Speaker Perks worth over $2,000!

Apply to Speak Today!

 https://form.jotform.com/250646617740156

NOVEMBER 6-7 2025 | LAS VEGAS, NEVADA

PURELY HEAVENLY

How *Lovely LaGuerre* is Redefining Luxury, Leadership & Inner Radiance Through Beauty

In a world where beauty is often filtered and fabricated, Lovely LaGuerre dares to redefine it. As the founder of Pure Heavenly Hair and Beauty Boutique and a multi-time international bestselling author, she is on a mission far deeper than just glamour. She's building a legacy—one infused with confidence, empowerment, and divine self-expression.

With a brand rooted in soul-centered beauty and purpose-driven leadership, Lovely doesn't just sell products—she curates transformation. I had the honor of sitting down with this powerhouse visionary to talk about her journey, her mission, and the radiant movement she's created through Pure Heavenly Hair and Beauty.

Q1. What inspired you to create Pure Heavenly Hair and Beauty Boutique, and what sets it apart in the beauty industry?

Lovely:
The driving force behind Pure Heavenly Hair and Beauty Boutique was born out of a deep passion for helping women feel beautiful, confident, and truly seen.

I envisioned creating more than just a beauty brand. I wanted to build a sanctuary where beauty meets empowerment. Every product, every strand, and every service we offer is intentionally curated to elevate not only appearance but self-worth.

What sets Pure Heavenly and Beauty apart is our vision, our purpose and our unwavering commitment to excellence, authenticity, and the customer experience. We don't just sell beauty, we craft confidence, and a reminder that every woman is worthy of feeling heavenly in her own skin. We blend style with substance, delivering high end, accessible beauty solutions that reflect modern sophistication and timeless elegance. Our beauty collections are created with care, innovation, designed to elevate and to celebrate every woman's divine beauty and provide tools to glow boldly, lead confidently, and unleash your inner beauty.

Our brand stands at the intersection of luxury, empowerment, and authenticity. This is more than beauty, it's a lifestyle. It's a legacy. And it's a love letter to every woman ready to rise in her glow.

Q2. Your brand beautifully emphasizes inclusivity and individuality. How do you ensure Pure Heavenly reflects and supports all forms of beauty?

Lovely:
At Pure Heavenly Hair and Beauty, inclusivity is not a trend, it's our truth. I founded this brand with the unwavering belief that beauty is boundless, and every woman deserves to see herself reflected in the products she uses and the brand she supports. We celebrate individuality by intentionally designing beauty experiences that honor all shades, shapes, styles, and stories.

From our diverse range of textures and tones to our wear-and-go wigs and inclusive makeup collections, every offering is thoughtfully crafted to embrace and enhance the uniqueness of every woman. We don't define beauty, we empower women to define it for themselves. That means listening to our community, representing them authentically in our visuals, and creating collections that reflect real life, real women, and real beauty.

At Pure Heavenly, we don't just support all forms of beauty, we elevate them. Because when a woman sees herself in our brand, she doesn't just feel beautiful she feels unstoppable.

Q3. What has been your favorite product to develop within your luxury line, and why does it hold special meaning to you?

Lovely:
It's my Bling Top Lipgloss

Without a doubt, it's our **Bling Top Lip Gloss.** A myriad of colors as you choose. It's more than just lipgloss, it's a statement. I created it with the vision of capturing that *instant confidence boost* you get when your lips shine just right. The sparkle, the texture, the packaging it's all about turning everyday glam into a luxurious moment.

What makes it so special to me is the intention behind it. I wanted every woman to feel like she's stepping into her spotlight the moment she applies it. Whether you're heading to a board room meeting, a fun night out, or just owning your day this gloss is a reminder that you *are the moment.* It's beauty, boldness, and boss energy in a single swipe.

Q4. How does Pure Heavenly Hair and Beauty embody the message *"Pure Confidence | Pure Beauty | Purely Heavenly You"*?

Lovely:
Our message is more than a tagline; it's the heartbeat of everything we do. *Pure Confidence | Pure Beauty | Purely Heavenly You* reflects our mission to empower every woman to feel confident in her own skin, to embrace her beauty without limits, and to rise into the highest, most radiant version of herself.

At Pure Heavenly Hair and Beauty, we believe confidence is the foundation of true beauty. That's why we create our luxury products that don't just enhance your look, they elevate how you feel. From our meticulously crafted wigs and extensions to our show stopping opulent beauty line, every offering is designed to celebrate individuality and help women express their power unapologetically
.

Pure Beauty means honoring the divine beauty that already exists within you. We don't believe in covering up, we believe in amplifying your glow. And *Purely Heavenly You* is our reminder that you don't need to fit anyone's mold. You were made to stand out, shine brighter, and walk boldly in your own light.

This brand is a movement. It's about giving women the luxury, the tools, and the love they deserve to feel beautiful authentically, confidently, purely heavenly.

Q5. Can you share a memorable moment or piece of feedback from a customer that deeply touched or inspired you?

Lovely:
One moment that will stay with me forever came from a woman who reached out after purchasing one of our Wear-and-Go Luxury Wigs. She shared she had been battling a serious illness and had lost her hair during treatment. For months, she didn't feel like herself. Her confidence was shattered. But when she wore our wig for the first time, she said something shifted and she saw herself again.

She shares, *"This wig didn't just give me back my hair, it gave me back my identity, my strength, and my joy. I felt beautiful again."*

That message brought me to tears. It reminded me exactly why I created Pure Heavenly. Beauty is so much more than what we see in the mirror it's about how we feel when we look at ourselves. It's about the power of being seen, valued, and restored.

That woman's courage and vulnerability inspired me deeply. And every time I receive new feedback, a smile in a photo, or a message saying, *"You helped me feel like me again,"* it reminds me that this is more than a business, it's a divine purpose.

Q6. What role does conscious beauty and self-care play in the Pure Heavenly experience, and why is that important to you as a Stylish CEO?

Lovely:
Conscious beauty and self-care are the soul of the Pure Heavenly experience. For me, it's never just about creating beautiful products. It's about creating intentional moments where women can pause, reconnect with themselves, and feel worthy of their own care and attention.

As a stylish CEO, I lead with the belief that true beauty radiates from within. That's why every piece of Pure Heavenly is designed not only to elevate your outer glow, but to nurture your spirit. From the luxurious feel of our wigs and extensions to the empowering confidence that comes with a swipe of lipgloss, a stroke of our volumes holy grail mascara or the perfect finish with each of our opulent beauty collections is an invitation to indulge, and honor yourself and to stand in your power.

Conscious beauty is about choosing products that align with your values, your lifestyle, and your well-being. It's about knowing that luxury doesn't have to be rushed or superficial; it can be soulful, healing, and transformative.

That's what I want every woman to experience when she shops with us. I want her to feel celebrated, not just styled. Seen, not just sold to. Because in this world of constant movement, self-care isn't a luxury, it's a necessity. And when a woman invests in herself body, mind, and spirit she becomes unshakable and unstoppable.

At Pure Heavenly, we don't just create beauty. We create space for women to rise.

Q7. Your boutique offers more than just products—it's a lifestyle. What are some rituals or daily practices you recommend for women to reconnect with their inner beauty?

Lovely:
Absolutely. At Pure Heavenly, we believe that beauty begins from within and that self-care is a sacred act of self-connection.

I always say: before you pour into the world, you must first pour into yourself.

Here are some daily rituals I live by and encourage every woman in our Pure Heavenly community to embrace:

1. Start with stillness.
Begin your day in silence even for just five minutes. Breathe, affirm yourself, and set an intention. It's in those quiet moments that your spirit speaks the loudest.

2. Speak beauty into your day.
Affirm your glow. Look in the mirror and say something kind, something bold, something that reminds you of who you are. *"I am radiant. I am powerful. I am already enough."*

3. Honor your temple.
Whether it's applying your favorite Pure Heavenly lip gloss, styling your crown with one of our luxury wigs, or indulging in a skincare ritual do it with care. These aren't chores, they're acts of self-devotion.

4. Protect your energy.
Beauty isn't just about the external it's also about what you allow in. Choose peace. Set boundaries. Walk away from anything that dims your light.

5. End your day with gratitude.
Close your night with reflection. Write down three things you're proud of. Even on your hardest days, you're still growing. Still glowing.

To me, these rituals are more than habits; they are sacred spaces that every woman deserves. Pure Heavenly isn't just about what you wear on the outside. It's about creating a lifestyle where you feel seen, soft, strong, and fully aligned inside and out.

Because when a woman reconnects with her inner beauty, she becomes unstoppable.

Q8. As an international bestselling author of multiple books, how has your journey as a writer influenced your approach to entrepreneurship and leadership?

Lovely:
Writing has always been my soul's blueprint. It's how I breathe life into vision, anchor truth into purpose, and transform experience into impact.

As an international bestselling author, storytelling became more than a gift; it became my compass. Each book I've written has taught me how to lead with empathy, build with boldness, and serve with intention. My journey as a writer taught me to embrace the power of authenticity, and that same authenticity shapes how I show up as a leader and entrepreneur.

Entrepreneurship, to me, is the continuation of the story I've just told through service, strategy, and legacy building. The discipline of writing sitting with silence, pushing through resistance, rewriting when needed mirrors the very heart of business leadership. It requires vision, courage, and a deep connection to purpose.

Writing showed me that words hold weight. And when used with clarity and conviction, they can shift perspectives, open hearts, and ignite movements. That understanding became the heartbeat of my leadership style. I don't just build businesses, I build experiences that tell a story, transform lives, and inspire women to step into their own power.

Through *Lovely Inspire You*, I've created more than a brand. I've created a movement rooted in storytelling, authenticity, and elevation.

LOVELY
LAGUERRE
BEST SELLING AUTHOR

Every chapter of my writing journey has brought me closer to this mission: to lead with purpose, create with passion, and help others rise boldly into their own greatness.

Q9. What are some recurring themes in your writing, and how do they reflect your personal values or the mission behind Pure Heavenly?

Lovely:
As a storyteller, I believe words have the power to heal, liberate, and awaken purpose. I write to remind women that they are not meant to shrink, they are meant to shine, even in the aftermath of their hardest seasons. My work often explores what it means to rise from the ashes, to reclaim your identity, and to wear your story like a crown.

That same essence lives within Pure Heavenly. This brand is an extension of my pen; it's where elegance meets empowerment. Every product is a love letter to women who dare to live boldly, look radiant, and lead with authenticity. Whether I'm crafting and sharing my story or curating a luxury beauty experience, the message is the same: **you are worthy, you are powerful, and you are already enough.**

Q10. Do you find a connection between storytelling and beauty? How does telling your story and encouraging others to do the same amplify empowerment?

Lovely:
Yes, without a doubt. For me, storytelling *is* beauty. It's the purest form of expression, the most intimate reflection of who we are, where we've been, and the power we carry within. Just as beauty reveals itself through radiance, storytelling reveals itself through truth. They are both sacred acts of self-recognition.

When I share my story, I'm not just recalling events, I'm reclaiming my voice, honoring my journey, and turning my past into purpose.

And through Pure Heavenly Hair and Beauty, I've woven that same philosophy into every product, every message, and every moment we create. Our brand exists at the intersection of identity and elevation where beauty is no longer defined by the world's standards but by the stories we dare to own.

True beauty isn't about perfection it's about presence. It's about the woman who shows up, scars and all, still choosing to shine. And that's why storytelling is so powerful. It transforms silence into strength. It turns vulnerability into visibility. It reminds every woman that she is seen, worthy, and never alone.

When a woman tells her story whether in a book, through her personal style, or with the confidence to wear her crown boldly she unlocks something timeless. She reclaims her narrative. She redefines beauty on her own terms. And she becomes a mirror for other women to rise.

At Pure Heavenly, we believe beauty should reflect your soul, not just your surface. That's why our mission is rooted in more than luxury, it's rooted in legacy. Every wig, every gloss, every intentional experience we offer is designed to help women walk in their full truth. We're here to elevate the beauty industry by honoring individuality, embracing authenticity, and celebrating their personal power in every story.

Because when a woman owns her story, she becomes unstoppable. And that kind of beauty? That's purely heavenly.

Q11. What message do you hope readers walk away with after engaging with your books or your brand?

Lovely:
My deepest hope is that every woman who reads my books or experiences my brand walks away with one undeniable truth: *She is worthy. She is powerful. And she is already enough.* Through my writing, I invite readers into a space of truth, healing, and self-discovery. I don't write to impress, I write to impact. I share my journey, the highs, the heartbreaks, the breakthroughs so other women can see themselves reflected in the pages and be reminded of their own strength.

I want my readers to feel seen, heard, and empowered to rise into their full potential.

And with *Pure Heavenly Hair and Beauty*, that mission continues only now it's translated into every product, every touchpoint, and every experience we create. Our brand is a mirror that reflects back confidence, boldness, and inner beauty. I want women to feel radiant not because of what they put on but because of what's awakened within them. Whether someone picks up one of my books or unwraps one of our luxury products, I want them to walk away with a sense of power, peace, and possibility. I want them to know that beauty isn't something they chase, it's something they *already are.*

Because when a woman begins to believe in her worth, she becomes unstoppable. And if my work through words or beauty can help her remember that, then I've done what I was called to do.

You are the Masterpiece and the Muse, the Author and the Icon and it's your Time to Shine.

Q12. With so many achievements under your belt Entrepreneur, Wealth Creator, and Commercial Real Estate what advice would you give to aspiring women entrepreneurs and writers who want to walk in purpose and power?

Lovely:
Start bold. Stay intentional. Own every room you walk into.

My advice is simple, but sacred: **start before you're ready, and never apologize for your vision.** You don't need permission to walk in your calling, you just need the courage to trust it. As women, we've been conditioned to wait for the *"perfect time,"* but purpose doesn't wait. Purpose *pushes.* It stretches you. It pulls you toward a version of yourself you haven't even met yet and that's the beauty of becoming.

I built success across beauty, wellness, publishing, and real estate not because I had all the answers, but because I refused to shrink. From launching my luxury beauty brand, writing bestselling books, leading in wellness, and investing in a real estate portfolio, every move was rooted in purpose.

To the woman ready to rise: stop waiting for perfect timing. Build the brand. Write the book. Buy the building. Your vision is valid, and your voice has value. Create boldly. Lead with intention. And understand that wealth is more than money, it's mindset, legacy, and impact.

Every time you choose to show up for your dream, you give another woman the courage to do the same. That's power. That's the purpose. And that's what I live to embody through business, beauty, and every story I tell.

Happy Reading and Always Be Kind!

Connect With Lovely

www.pureheavenlyhair.com
www.lovelysellsvegas.com
www.instagram.com/pureheavenlyhair
www.twitter.com/Heavenly_Pure
www.facebook.com/share/1Bau9f8Ld6
www.in.pinterest.com/pureheavenly/wig-products

UNSHAKABLE WOMAN:

Lead with Energy, Not Exhaustion

By Sonya McDonald

For years, I pushed myself relentlessly, believing that hard work and perseverance were the keys to success. As a registered nurse with over three decades of experience, I was no stranger to long hours and high stress. However, I often ignored the signals my body was sending me, dismissing the fatigue and discomfort as mere side effects of a demanding career. Living with Rheumatoid Arthritis and Fibromyalgia for over sixteen years, I became adept at masking my pain and soldiering on. I told myself that slowing down was not an option, that my patients and colleagues depended on me. This mindset led me to a breaking point, a virus that landed me in the hospital, struggling to breathe.

It was in that hospital bed, with my body betraying me, that I had a profound realization: I could no longer afford to neglect my own well-being. This health crisis was my wake-up call, forcing me to confront the unsustainable pace I had set for myself. The body truly does keep the score and sends us red lights when we push too hard until we are completely emotionally and physically exhausted. Emerging from this experience, I was determined to find a better way, not just for myself, but for the countless women I knew were facing similar battles.

I developed the E.N.E.R.G.Y. Code, a framework designed to help women lead with purpose without sacrificing their health.

E – Eliminate what drains you. Recognize the commitments and relationships that deplete your energy and set boundaries to protect your well-being.

N – Nourish your whole being. Prioritize self-care by addressing your physical, emotional, and mental health needs. This includes adopting healthy habits, seeking support, and allowing yourself time to rest.

E – Expand what fuels you. Engage in activities and pursuits that bring you joy and fulfillment. Invest your time and energy in what aligns with your passions and values.

R – Reconnect with your purpose. Reflect on your core values and what drives you. Align your daily actions with your deeper purpose to create a sense of meaning and direction. G – Ground yourself in stillness. Incorporate moments of mindfulness and reflection into your routine. This practice helps you stay centered and responsive rather than reactive to life's challenges.

Y – You come first. Understand that prioritizing your health and well-being is not selfish; it is essential. By taking care of yourself, you are better equipped to serve and lead others effectively. Implementing the E.N.E.R.G.Y. Code really transformed my life. I learned that true strength lies not in pushing through at all costs but in recognizing when to pause and care for oneself. This shift allowed me to lead more authentically and compassionately.

Inspired by this journey, I authored my upcoming first Solo book, Unshakable, set to release this summer. In it, I go deeper into the principles of the E.N.E.R.G.Y. Code and share strategies for women to lead with confidence. It's a powerful blueprint for the woman who's tired of just surviving, and ready to rise. I finally understood that real strength isn't pushing through pain. It's pausing, pivoting, and protecting what matters most: your peace, your health, your light. If you're done living on empty and ready to lead with pure intention, this is your moment. If you're ready to break free from the cycle of burnout and embrace a life of energy and purpose, I invite you to connect with me. Scan QR code and Visit me at www.sonyamcdonald.com to learn more about my coaching and speaking engagements. Ignite your light and transform your life.

Connect With Sonya

www.sonyamcdonald.com
www.facebook.com/sonya.mcdonald.96
www.instagram.com/sonyamcdonald_
www.linkedin.com/in/sonya-mcdonald-rn-bsn-bcc-7786521b9

SHE RISES
STUDIOS

JOIN THE SRS COMMUNITY

WHERE WOMEN RISE TOGETHER!

Connect. Empower. Thrive. Whether you're an entrepreneur, professional, or simply seeking inspiration, **this is your space to grow!**

* Daily Motivation
* Expert Insights
* Sisterhood & Support

You don't have to do it alone—let's rise together!

JOIN NOW!

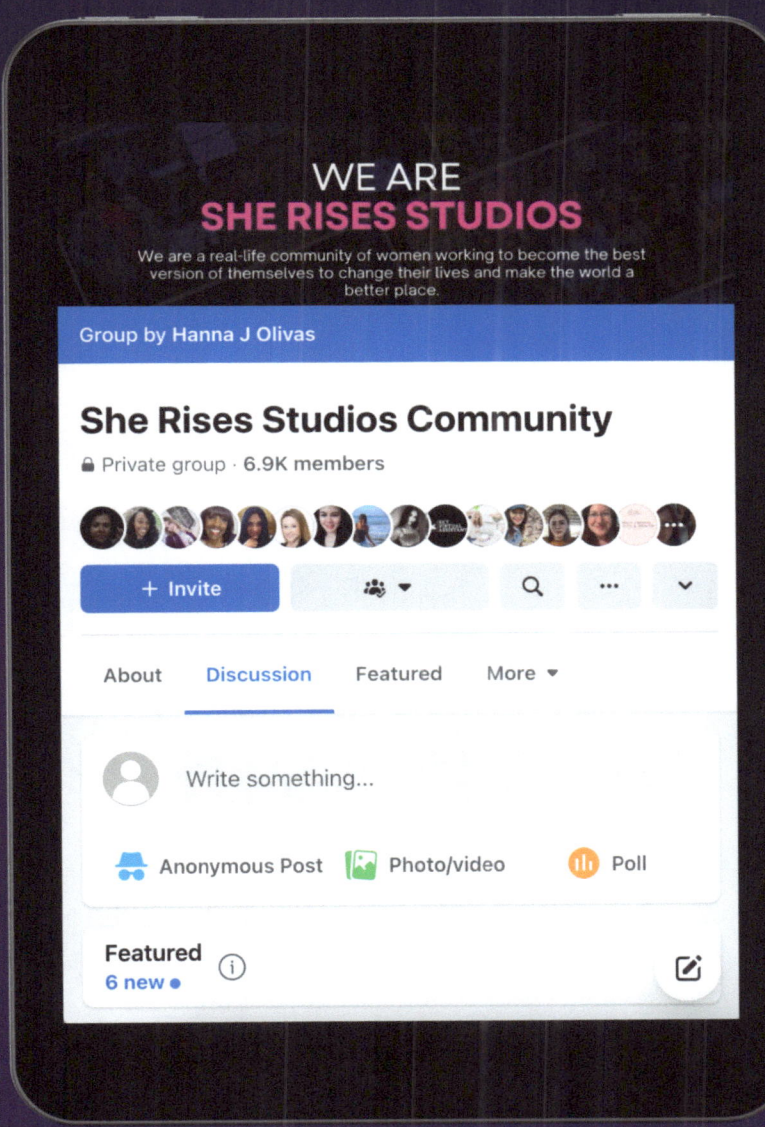

www.bit.ly/srscommunitygroup   www.sherisesstudios.com

WHEN BEAUTY IS A BYPRODUCT OF HEALING:

The Mental Health Benefits of Brazilian Lymphatic Drainage

By Carrie Riley

We've all heard the phrase, *"When you look good, you feel good."* But what if the reverse is just as true? At Cincinnati Massage for Mental Health, we've seen again and again how feeling good in your body. Feeling grounded, calm, and connected can change the way you carry yourself through the world. There's a kind of glow that doesn't come from a product or a procedure. It comes from within.

That inner radiance is what makes Brazilian Lymphatic Drainage Massage so special. While it's well known for visibly sculpting the body and reducing puffiness, the deeper benefits often go unspoken. Yes, it helps reduce bloating and inflammation, but more importantly, it helps you reconnect with your body in a way that supports lasting beauty from the inside out.

The Healing Rhythm of Lymphatic Touch

Brazilian Lymphatic Drainage Massage is very different from a typical spa massage or deep tissue work. It's a gentle, intentional technique that uses rhythmic strokes, myofascial release, and light compression to support the lymphatic system, which is your body's natural detox pathway. When the lymphatic system is functioning well, it helps move fluid toward the lymph nodes, clearing out inflammation, toxins, and cellular waste that can build up due to stress, illness, or post-surgical recovery.

Another important part of the treatment is the consistent rocking motion used throughout the session. That rhythm gently activates the parasympathetic nervous system. This is the part of your body responsible for rest, digestion, and emotional regulation. When it's active, the body can begin to repair itself. And for many clients, this is when they take their first full breath in weeks.

A Ritual for Radiance and Resilience

What makes this massage so powerful is that it blends beauty and wellness into one calming, effective experience. It may start with visible results, but the effect it has on the nervous system is what supports lasting radiance.

Studies suggest that this type of massage can improve heart rate variability, which is a sign of how well the body handles stress. Higher variability is associated with better sleep, emotional resilience, and fewer symptoms of anxiety or depression.

It's also been shown to help improve vagal tone. The vagus nerve is a major communication line between the brain and the body, and it plays a key role in mood regulation, digestion, inflammation, and even skin clarity. When the vagus nerve is healthy and responsive, people tend to feel calmer, more grounded, and more emotionally steady.

In a world that's always asking us to do more and push harder, Brazilian Lymphatic Drainage offers something very different. It gives you the chance to slow down and come back to yourself. What begins as a beauty treatment becomes a wellness ritual.

Our Clients Say It Best

Many clients describe this massage as a turning point. Not just for their body, but for their overall well-being. They report feeling lighter, not just in terms of swelling, but in their mood and mindset. There's often a shift in energy and a sense of clarity that continues long after the session ends.

It's also not uncommon for clients to say this is one of the only treatments where they're able to fully drop in. The soft rhythm and supportive environment invite a kind of presence that's hard to find in everyday life. That connection to breath, sensation, and awareness can be deeply healing, especially for those dealing with trauma, chronic stress, or emotional overwhelm.

Beauty as a Byproduct of Self-Connection

At its core, Brazilian Lymphatic Drainage Massage is about embodiment. That means being present in your own body and feeling at home there. For people living with anxiety, recovering from surgery, or struggling with body image, that kind of presence can feel unfamiliar or even uncomfortable at first.

But with consistent care, things begin to shift. Muscles soften. Breathing slows. Thoughts get quieter. And gradually, the body starts to feel safe again. When that happens, beauty starts to emerge naturally. Not because it's being forced, but because it's being lived.

A Practice of Inner and Outer Renewal

Whether you're preparing for a special occasion, healing after surgery, or simply needing to reconnect with yourself, Brazilian Lymphatic Drainage Massage offers more than a temporary glow. It's a practice that honors your body's wisdom and helps you come back into alignment with your own rhythm.

When you feel good, it shows. Your skin brightens. Your posture shifts. Your presence becomes magnetic.

At Cincinnati Massage for Mental Health, we are honored to be part of that transformation. Our work isn't about fixing or perfecting. It's about reconnecting. To your breath, your body, and your inner calm. Because that's where real beauty begins.

Connect With Carrie

www.MentalHealthMassage.com
www.instagram.com/cincymentalhealthmassage
www.facebook.com/MentalHealthMassageTherapy
www.linkedin.com/company/cincinnati-massage-for-mental-health

FLAWED YET FABULOUS:

How Your Unique Talents Make You Invaluable

By Michele Gunn

Your flaws are part of what makes you extraordinary. We are all uniquely created with strengths, talents, and even perceived flaws that contribute to our value. Together, we will explore how our uniqueness makes us invaluable. You will also find tips on recognizing and using your gifts effectively.

The Beauty of Imperfection

Society often pressures people to fit a mold, yet our differences are what make us special. It starts right from birth! There are expectations on how you should look, act and develop. There is no embracing your uniqueness! As we age, we are compared to other babies as well as charts on where we should be in development. Toddlers are told how to behave and that certain behaviors are *"not nice."* There is a difference between acceptable behaviors and unacceptable behaviors when it comes to safety and hurting others. Let's face it. Each one of us humans is different. We don't fit a mold. As we grow and develop into teenagers and then adults, many of us *"hide"* parts of who we are.

For example, when I was in elementary school, a teacher put tape over my mouth during class because I talked too much. I was called nosy because I enjoyed being in the know. Both of these things stifled my development and my natural talents for communication and information gathering.

Recognizing Your Unique Talents and Strengths

Everyone has God-given talents, but many people struggle to recognize them. Here are some practical ways to discover your gifts:
- Reflect on what excites you or comes naturally.
- Consider what others appreciate about you.
- Take assessments like CliftonStrengths® to gain deeper insights.
- Work with a coach to help you uncover your unique goodness.

Self-reflection and journaling are tools to track moments of success and fulfillment. You can then look for patterns to uncover your strengths. Strengths, when not used properly, can be disguised as flaws or weaknesses. A good coach can help you discern that.

Aiming Your Talents for Impact

It is important to direct your talents toward meaningful goals. Much like a musician fine-tuning their instrument, if your skills and talents aren't fine tuned, you will not achieve the desired results. Follow these tips to apply your strengths effectively:
- Align talents with a purpose or mission
- Surround yourself with people who complement your abilities.
- Continue learning and growing in your strengths.

Remember that talents are not just for personal success, but for serving and uplifting others.

Overcoming Doubt and Embracing Your Worth

We are taught from a young age to be more concerned with what is wrong with us than what is right. We are taught to second guess our decisions and to be critical of who we are, what we do and how we do it. We are ingrained with self-doubt and the fear of not being enough. It becomes part of our thinking process. Our mind begins to control us with negativity, stopping us with constant fear of failure or simply not being *"good enough."*

It's time to take control. Know your worth. Do not allow anyone (especially yourself) to diminish your value. Use your talents to serve and achieve success.

You are not flawed. You are fabulous!

When we embrace our whole selves, we step into our true calling. The world doesn't need a perfect version of you. It doesn't need more people that are molded to fit the norm. It needs the real, uniquely gifted, beautifully imperfect you. The world needs the you that you were created to be.

Connect With Michele

www.michelegunn.com
www.linkedin.com/in/michelegunn
www.facebook.com/michele.jonasgunn
www.instagram.com/michelegunn1

EMPOWERED VOICES:

Leading Boldly with Authenticity

By Carol Salvadori

Have you ever felt the pressure to conform in order to succeed? In a world where voices can easily get lost amidst a sea of sameness, authentic leadership is not simply a choice—it's a necessity. The journey to finding and embracing our true selves is a powerful one, capable of not only transforming our own paths but also inspiring those around us.

As the founder of LEADLoud Academy, my journey began with a profound realization: true impact comes from being boldly authentic. There was a time when I navigated complex professional landscapes, trying to fit into moulds that were never designed for me. It was only when I started to listen to my inner voice that I began to understand the true meaning of leadership. Embracing my real self allowed me to connect on a deeper level with those around me, building trust and fostering collaboration.

Authenticity in leadership is crucial for several reasons. Firstly, it builds a foundation of trust. When leaders are transparent and genuine, they create an environment where team members feel seen and valued. This, in turn, enhances engagement and performance. Secondly, authentic leaders inspire creativity and innovation by encouraging others to bring their true selves to the table. A diverse mix of perspectives leads to rich ideas that drive success.

But how can you start embracing authenticity in your leadership journey? It begins with self-reflection. Take time to understand your values, strengths, and areas you're passionate about. Create a vision for how you want to show up as a leader and align your actions with these core beliefs. Secondly, practice active listening —not just to those around you, but also to your inner voice. It will guide you toward decisions and actions that resonate with your true self.

LEADLoud Academy is dedicated to supporting individuals on this path. We believe that each leader's unique voice is their most powerful tool. Our programs are designed to amplify these voices, providing the skills and confidence needed to lead with authenticity and impact. Through a blend of mentorship, community, and innovative methodologies, we empower leaders to stand out and thrive.

You possess a voice that is both unique and powerful. Embrace it, nurture it, and watch as it transforms not only your leadership but the world around you. At LEADLoud Academy, we believe that when leaders speak authentically, they ignite change. So step forward with confidence and let your true voice shine— because bold leaders with authentic voices are the ones who truly win.

Connect With Carol

www.linkedin.com/in/leadloudacademy
Free E-Book: www.leadloudacademy.mykajabi.com/opt-in-d401b2c7-5292-4dba-9924-1f8912dd064d
www.leadloudacademy.com

The SHE RISES STUDIOS
PODCAST

TUNE IN. RISE UP. THRIVE.

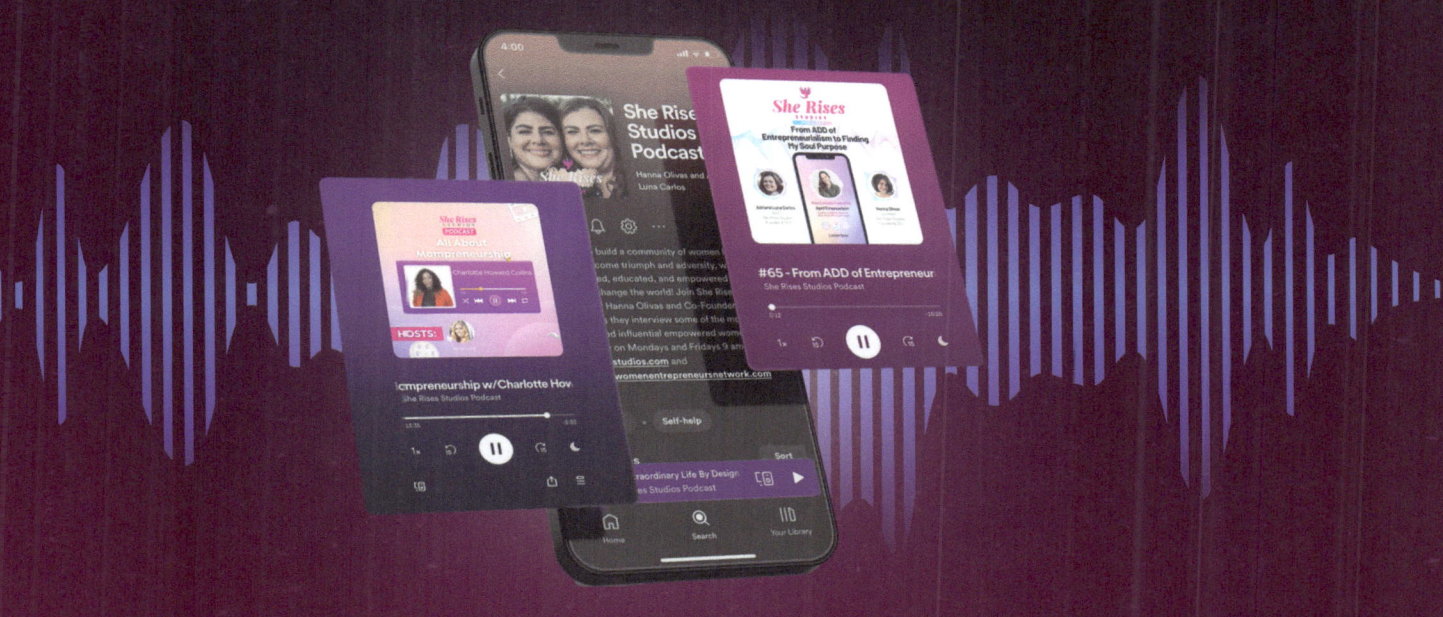

Looking for **real conversations** that inspire, empower, and ignite your potential? The **SRS Podcast** is where women like you come to **learn, grow, and rise!**

Join us for powerful **interviews with trailblazing entrepreneurs, thought leaders, and everyday women** who have turned obstacles into opportunities. Our episodes dive into:

➢ **Breaking through self-doubt** and stepping into confidence
➢ **Building a thriving business** with purpose and passion
➢ **Mastering work-life balance** without guilt
➢ **Leveling up your mindset, health, and career**
➢ **Finding your true purpose and living boldly**

Each episode is packed with **real stories, expert insights, and actionable strategies** to help you take your life to the next level. **This isn't just a podcast—it's your roadmap to success!**

SUBSCRIBE NOW AND START YOUR JOURNEY TO EMPOWERMENT!

By Tamsyn Cornelius

ANSWERING THE CALL:

Embracing Your Creative Purpose

Creative entrepreneurship often feels less like a choice and more like a calling—an unshakable force pulling you toward self-expression. No matter how much life tries to reroute you, the desire to create always finds its way back. For me, art and creativity came as a whisper in the background of my busy life as a mom, a writer, and a freelancer. Until one day, it became impossible to ignore.

Rekindling the Creative Flame

For many years, creativity took a backseat to the demands of work and family. My days revolved around a bustling copywriting business and raising two children, while my passion for painting was reduced to small bursts of craft projects and home decor. But in 2020, when the world hit pause, I was forced to reflect. I asked myself: What gifts have I been neglecting? What do I truly have to offer the world?

So, I picked up a paintbrush again and what started as a personal challenge—to create one painting a month—quickly evolved into painting every week, then every day. Each brushstroke reignited something inside me. Soon, I found myself selling my work, creating custom commissions, and transforming a corner of my home into a dedicated art studio.

The Journey from *'Stuck'* to *'Creator'*

Art is more than just a pastime—it's a way of making sense of the world, a means of storytelling, and a conduit for deeper connection. Yet, many aspiring artists struggle to take that first step. If you feel creatively stuck, perhaps it is time to reignite your passion and pursue your calling. Here are some considerations...

1. Make The Time

Life is busy, but if you have a passion, you must nurture it. Block out time in your schedule to create, even if it's just an hour a week. Learn, practice, and explore different techniques. Attend workshops, take online courses, and allow yourself the space to grow.

2. Stop Comparing Yourself to Others

In a world of social media perfection, it's easy to feel inadequate. But comparison is the enemy of creativity.

Instead of measuring yourself against others, focus on improving your skills and enjoying the process. Every artist has a unique journey—embrace yours.

3. Share Your Work with the World

Fear of judgment holds many creatives back. But art is meant to be seen, felt, and experienced. Start by sharing your work with friends and family. Then, take the leap—set up an online portfolio, display your pieces at local markets, or showcase your work on social media.

4. Connect Your Creativity to a Greater Purpose

Why do you create? Understanding your deeper motivation fuels perseverance. Whether it's self-expression, storytelling, or faith-driven artistry, anchoring your work in purpose gives it meaning beyond aesthetics.

Building a Creative Life

Today, my art is more than just paintings on a canvas—it's a way to inspire, connect, and encourage others. I have since added retreat curation to my business, creating a gathering place for creativity, where I host reflective retreats and workshops, paint parties, and one-on-one mentorship sessions. I love watching people's faces light up when they create something they never thought possible.

Art has a way of awakening something dormant inside us—a forgotten passion, a buried dream, a spark of purpose. If you feel the pull toward creativity, don't ignore it. Lean in, explore, and create. The world needs what only you can bring.

Connect With Tamsyn

www.tamsyncornelius.com
www.tceditorialservices.co.za

THE FULLEST STORIES:

A Revolution in Radical Reinvention

By Stephanie Dauble

What if the life you've been waiting for has been waiting on you to claim it? What if every detour, blindside, and hard-earned lesson was never meant to break you--but to awaken the dormant brilliance that was destined to be unleashed?

This is the heartbeat of The Fullest Stories: a movement for those who refuse to let their past define their future, who know that reinvention isn't just possible or inevitable—it's our responsibility.

It's for the ones who have been underestimated, those who have walked through fire and emerged as something unrecognizable—more luminous, formidable, and unyielding--unwilling to shrink to fit a life that no longer serves them. It's for those who know that the glow-up isn't just about aesthetics; it's about unapologetic boldness.

Because here's the truth: the best stories aren't just told. They're lived fully.

More Than a Brand—A Reckoning

Some people use trauma as an excuse to stay small. The Fullest Stories is a rallying cry for those who refuse to.

We are the architects of our own expansion. We are proof that heartbreak, failure, and reinvention are not endpoints but invitations—opportunities to rise so fully into our greatness that even we can't believe our own audacity.

This isn't about passive inspiration. It's about active transformation. This is for the woman who walked away from the relationship that dimmed her light and built a life so vibrant it made her old self unrecognizable. For the man who left behind the golden handcuffs of corporate success to chase the thing that set his soul on fire. For the visionary who took their pain and turned it into purpose.

We don't just talk about reinvention. We embody it.

The Luxury of Expansion

Luxury isn't just about designer labels or five-star getaways—it's the ability to choose. To rewrite your own story. To build a life that feels as good on the inside as it looks on the outside.

At The Fullest Stories, we believe in living with intention. If we drink the champagne, we savor it. If we travel, we immerse ourselves in cultures, not just destinations. If we love, we love expansively—not out of fear, obligation, or habit, but with the full knowing that we are worthy of relationships that elevate. And, if we build, we create legacies, not just careers.

The glow-up isn't about things. It's about energy. It's about stepping into a version of yourself so fully realized that you no longer recognize the person who once settled for anything less than their own divinity.

The Invitation

This isn't about changing who you are. It's about a self-reckoning so honest, so absolute, that looking back is no longer an option— a return to who you've always been before the world tried to convince you to play by manufactured rules designed to keep you small.

One extraordinary life is all we get. Will you wait for life to force your hand, or will you seize it now on your terms?

It's go time!

Connect With Stephanie

www.medium.com/@stephanie.dauble
@thefulleststories

GET YOUR COPY NOW

Celebrate the power of women through inspiring stories and insights.

From Surviving to Thriving
Gina Stockdall

Shifting Narratives
Anita Comisky and Michelle Belloit

Stepping into Wadzi:
Lessons from my life
Wadzanai Garwe

Garden to Kitchen Planner
Ines Batterton

Invisible to Visible
Julie Lavia

Unlearn the Crap and Level Up
Kathy Baldwin

The Two *Most Popular* *Fat Loss* Eating *Strategies*

By Teri Katzenberger

- Intermittent Fasting (IF)
- Six Small Meals a Day

Both have their loyal fans. But which one is more effective? And more importantly, which one fits your lifestyle and goals?

Let's take a closer look:
- **Intermittent Fasting.** Intermittent fasting is all about when you eat—not necessarily what you eat. This strategy involves cycling between periods of eating and fasting.

Some popular IF schedules include:
- **16:8 Method** – Fast for 16 hours, eat during an 8-hour window
- **5:2 Method** – Eat normally five days a week, restrict calories for two

Pros:
- Can help with appetite control
- May improve insulin sensitivity
- Often leads to reduced calorie intake naturally

Things to consider:
- May not work well if you prefer to eat breakfast
- Energy dips or hunger pangs may happen early on
- Can take time to adjust

How to Eat for the Best Results
When it comes to fat loss, food matters —a lot. But it's not just what you eat that counts. How much and how often you eat also play a huge role in your results.

That's why the question of how to eat for optimal fat loss is one I hear all the time from clients. So let's break down two of the most talked-about strategies and figure out which one might be the right fit for YOU.

Intermittent Fasting
Intermittent fasting is an eating strategy that cycles between periods of eating and periods of fasting.

The focus isn't necessarily on what you eat, but when you eat.

There are several popular methods
- **16:8 method** – Fast for 16 hours, eat within an 8-hour window (ex: 12 PM to 8 PM).
- **5:2 method** – Eat normally for five days, then restrict calories to around 500–600 for two non-consecutive days.
- **Eat-Stop-Eat** – A full 24-hour fast once or twice per week.

Many people find that intermittent fasting helps with appetite control, better digestion, and even mental clarity. It can also naturally reduce your calorie intake without counting every bite.

Some people feel great skipping breakfast, while others feel sluggish or irritable. The key is listening to your body and finding a rhythm that works with your lifestyle.

Six Small Meals

On the flip side, the six-small-meals-a-day strategy encourages you to eat every 2–3 hours to keep your metabolism humming and hunger at bay.

Each meal is smaller and typically balanced with protein, healthy fats, and complex carbs.

This approach can:
- Help stabilize blood sugar levels
- Prevent overeating at mealtimes
- Support steady energy throughout the day

People who thrive on routine and love structure often do well with this method. However, for some, it can feel like you're constantly planning or eating—so it must be something you can realistically maintain.

So...Which One is Right for You?

What to consider:
- **Your lifestyle:** Are you constantly on the go, or do you have time to prep and plan meals?
- **Your body's signals:** Do you feel energized by fasting or do you need fuel more frequently?
- **Your goals:** Is your focus fat loss, muscle gain, energy, or just feeling better day to day?

Ultimately, both strategies can work—if you stay consistent, eat quality food, and avoid overeating (under-eating) during your eating windows.

Bottom Line

There's no one-size-fits-all when it comes to eating for fat loss. The best results come when you choose a method that fits your life, supports your goals, and makes you feel GOOD—physically and mentally.

Need help figuring out what works best for you? Let's chat—I've helped dozens of clients find their sweet spot, and I'd love to help you too.

Connect With Teri

www.livewellnow.academy
www.livewellnowacademy.com
www.facebook.com/TeriKatzenberger
www.instagram.com/TeriKatzenberger

GET YOUR COPY NOW

Celebrate the power of women through inspiring stories and insights.

How I Unlearned My Crap
Kathy Baldwin

Stepping Up to Lead
Annabelle and India Beckwith

Redefined Flourishing In
Life While Becoming Wife
Breanna James

Redefining You
Amanda Cahill

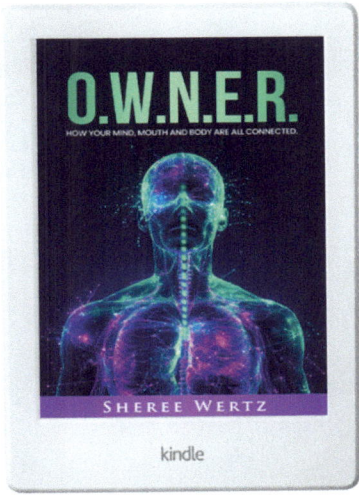

O.W.N.E.R.
Sheree Wertz

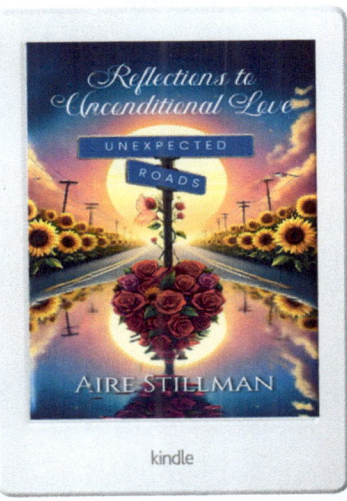

Reflections to Unconditional Love
Aire Stillman

LORI *HARDER:*

*Empowering Women Through Fitness,
Self-Care, and Self-Love*

In a world where the pressures to achieve perfection often overshadow the importance of inner peace, Lori Harder's approach to wellness and self-care stands as a powerful reminder of the transformative effects of self-love. As a fitness expert, motivational speaker, and author, Lori has spent her career empowering women to tap into their full potential by focusing on the profound connection between self-care, fitness, and personal development. She doesn't just preach wellness—she embodies it, inspiring countless women to embrace a holistic approach to health that nurtures both body and soul.

As we step into May, a month that celebrates renewal and mental health, Lori's message of self-love is a timely reminder that beauty is about more than just outer appearance—it's about the deep, nurturing work we do within. Her work focuses on helping women cultivate the confidence that comes from embracing their worth, fueling their bodies with intention, and prioritizing their mental and emotional well-being. It's a message that aligns perfectly with this month's theme of radiating confidence, beauty, and self-care.

Lori's own journey to wellness and self-love wasn't always a straightforward path. Like many of us, she faced her own struggles with self-doubt, insecurity, and body image issues. But rather than succumbing to the pressures of society's beauty standards, she chose to embark on a journey of personal development that would ultimately change the course of her life. Lori's story is a testament to the power of embracing self-care, not as an afterthought, but as a cornerstone of confidence and success.

Her approach to fitness is grounded in the belief that it's not just about sculpting a certain body type—it's about honoring your body as a tool for self-love and empowerment. Lori emphasizes the importance of finding joy in movement, not as a punishment for eating or as a way to shrink yourself, but as a celebration of your body's strength and resilience. Through her fitness programs and motivational speaking, she teaches women to embrace their bodies in all their forms, to appreciate what they can do, and to move with intention and gratitude.

But fitness is only one aspect of Lori's holistic approach to wellness. At the heart of her message is the idea that self-care is essential to mental health. She often speaks about the importance of carving out time for yourself—whether that's through meditation, journaling, or simply taking a few quiet moments to reflect. She encourages women to let go of guilt and prioritize their own needs, which is often the first step in reclaiming confidence. Self-care, Lori believes, isn't a luxury—it's a necessity for maintaining balance and happiness.

One of Lori's key teachings is that true confidence comes from within. Confidence is not about looking a certain way or achieving external validation; it's about cultivating a deep sense of self-worth that radiates outwards. Through her books, speaking engagements, and coaching, Lori encourages women to do the inner work necessary to build lasting confidence. She promotes the idea that by investing in ourselves—through self-care practices, personal development, and fitness—we can create a life that reflects our highest potential.

As a motivational speaker, Lori also emphasizes the importance of mindset in achieving personal growth and wellness. She believes that our thoughts and beliefs are the foundation for everything we do, and by shifting our mindset, we can transform our lives. Whether it's through a morning affirmations practice or by setting powerful intentions, Lori teaches women to reframe their thinking and break free from self-limiting beliefs. When we learn to believe in ourselves, we begin to act in ways that reflect that belief, opening doors to greater opportunities and experiences.

Lori's work is particularly impactful because it combines practical strategies with deep emotional healing. She meets women where they are, offering tools for self-love and growth while also providing a compassionate space for personal transformation. Whether she's teaching a fitness class, hosting a podcast, or guiding a meditation, Lori's presence radiates warmth, wisdom, and encouragement, making her a true leader in the wellness space.

As we celebrate Mental Health Awareness Month, Lori's message reminds us that mental health is a crucial aspect of beauty and well-being. Wellness is not just about looking good on the outside; it's about feeling good on the inside. It's about nourishing our minds, bodies, and spirits with kindness, care, and love. By prioritizing self-care, embracing fitness as a form of self-love, and doing the emotional work to build confidence, we can achieve a balanced, beautiful life that reflects our true selves.

So this May, as we embrace the theme of Radiate Confidence, take a page from Lori Harder's playbook. Invest in your self-care. Move with intention. Cultivate a mindset of abundance and self-worth. Because when you love and care for yourself—physically, mentally, and emotionally—you unlock the confidence to live a life that's truly in full bloom.

www.sherisesstudios.com

SELF-CARE IS SELF-LOVE:

Nurturing Your Inner Garden for Radiant Beauty and Unshakeable Confidence

By Grace Olayiwola

As the founder of ALGSTUDIOSTORE and ALGELYSIANFLAMESCO, my journey has been deeply intertwined with the profound understanding that true beauty and unwavering confidence blossom from the fertile ground of self-care. It's more than just bubble baths and face masks; it's a holistic approach to nurturing your mental, emotional, and physical well-being. Self-care, at its core, is an act of profound self-love – a conscious decision to prioritize your needs and cultivate a thriving inner landscape.

In our fast-paced world, it's easy to get caught up in the demands of daily life, often neglecting the very person who deserves our utmost care: ourselves. We pour energy into our careers, our families, and our responsibilities, sometimes leaving little in the reservoir for our own replenishment. This neglect can manifest in various ways – stress, anxiety, fatigue, a diminished sense of self-worth, and even physical ailments.

However, when we consciously choose self-care, we send a powerful message to ourselves: *"I am worthy of my own time, attention, and love."* This simple act of prioritization can have a transformative ripple effect, enhancing not only our mental wellness but also radiating outwards to impact our beauty, self-love, and overall confidence.

The Intricate Connection: Mental Wellness, Beauty, Self-Love, and Confidence

Consider a vibrant flower. Its beauty isn't solely determined by the color of its petals, but also by the health of its roots, the nourishment it receives, and the sunlight it basks in. Similarly, our external beauty is intrinsically linked to our internal state. When our minds are cluttered with stress and negativity, it often reflects on our skin, our posture, and our overall demeanor.

Mental wellness forms the bedrock of self-love. When we actively tend to our mental health, we cultivate a sense of inner peace and acceptance. This inner harmony allows us to see ourselves with greater compassion and kindness, fostering a deeper sense of self-love. As self-love flourishes, so too does our confidence. When we truly value and appreciate ourselves, we project an aura of self-assurance that is undeniably attractive.

Cultivating Your Inner Sanctuary: Mental Wellness Tips for Enhanced Well-being

As an advocate for holistic self-care, I believe in incorporating practices that nourish the mind and soul. Here are some mental wellness tips that can significantly enhance your beauty, self-love and overall confidence:

Embrace the Power of Mindfulness: In a world filled with distractions, cultivating mindfulness is like finding an anchor in a storm. Dedicate a few minutes each day to simply being present – focusing on your breath, your senses, or a guided meditation. This practice helps to quiet the mental chatter, reduce stress, and foster a greater sense of inner awareness.

Nourish Your Mind with Positive Input: Just as we are mindful of the food we consume; we should also be conscious of the information we absorb. Limit exposure to negativity, whether it's through news, social media, or toxic relationships. Instead, seek out uplifting content, inspiring books, and supportive connections that nourish your mind and spirit.

Practice Gratitude Daily: Cultivating an attitude of gratitude shifts our focus from what we lack to what we have. Take a few moments each day to reflect on the things you are grateful for, no matter how small. This simple practice can boost your mood, increase feelings of positivity, and enhance your overall sense of well-being.

Prioritize Quality Sleep: Sleep is not a luxury; it's a fundamental necessity for both our mental and physical health. Aim for 7-9 hours of quality sleep each night to allow your body and mind to rest and rejuvenate. Establish a relaxing bedtime routine to signal your body that it's time to wind down.

Move Your Body with Intention: Physical activity is not just about achieving a certain physique; it's a powerful tool for boosting mood, reducing stress, and increasing energy levels. Find activities you enjoy, whether it's dancing, yoga, walking in nature, or hitting the gym. Movement releases endorphins, which have mood-boosting effects and contribute to a greater sense of well-being.

Embrace Creative Expression: Engaging in creative activities, such as painting, writing, playing music, or crafting, can be incredibly therapeutic. It allows you to tap into your inner world, express your emotions, and experience a sense of flow and joy.

Set Healthy Boundaries: Learning to say *"no"* is an act of self-love. Setting boundaries protects your time, energy, and emotional well-being. It allows you to prioritize your needs and prevents you from feeling overwhelmed or resentful.

Seek Support When Needed: There is strength in vulnerability. If you are struggling with your mental health, don't hesitate to reach out to a therapist, counselor, or trusted friend or family member. Seeking support is a sign of self-awareness and a commitment to your well-being.

Practice Self-Compassion: Treat yourself with the same kindness and understanding you would offer a dear friend. Acknowledge your imperfections, learn from your mistakes, and forgive yourself. Self-compassion fosters a sense of inner acceptance and strengthens your self-love.

Engage Your Senses: Indulge in experiences that delight your senses. Light a scented candle, listen to calming music, savor a delicious meal, or spend time in nature. Engaging your senses can be grounding and bring moments of joy and relaxation.

Integrating Self-Care into Your Daily Rituals

Self-care doesn't need to be grand gestures; it's often the small, consistent acts that make the biggest difference. Integrate these mental wellness tips into your daily rituals. Perhaps you start your day with a few minutes of mindful breathing, take a short walk during your lunch break, or wind down in the evening with a calming cup of tea and a gratitude journal.

By consciously weaving self-care into the fabric of your life, you are actively nurturing your inner garden. As you tend to your mental well-being, you will witness a natural blossoming of your inner and outer beauty, a deepening of your self-love, and a radiant surge of confidence that emanates from within. Remember, self-care is not selfish; it is an essential act of self-love that allows you to thrive and shine your brightest.

It is an investment in the most important person in your life – you.

Connect With Grace

Instagram: @AlgstudioStore_LLC
www.algstudiostore.com
Instagram: @ALGelysianflames
www.algelysianflamesco.com

MEGAN
CRABB:

Empowering Women to Embrace Their Bodies and Mental Well-Being

In a world flooded with curated images of perfection, Megan Crabb—better known as Megan Jayne Crabbe—is a refreshing, bold voice of body positivity and self-love. With a mission to break beauty standards and empower individuals to embrace their bodies and mental well-being, Megan has become a beacon of confidence and self-acceptance for women everywhere. Through her advocacy, she helps others redefine what it means to feel beautiful and worthy, all while championing the importance of mental health.

As we celebrate Mental Health Awareness Month, Megan's work reminds us that true beauty is not about fitting into a mold set by society—it's about owning who we are and accepting ourselves exactly as we are. Her message is simple yet revolutionary: self-love isn't just a trendy concept; it's a necessary practice for cultivating lasting confidence and happiness. And in a time when beauty standards are constantly evolving and often unrealistic, Megan's voice stands as a powerful testament to the idea that beauty is diverse, fluid, and deeply personal.

Megan's journey to becoming a body positivity advocate and mental health champion began with her own struggles with body image and disordered eating. As a young woman, she grappled with societal pressures to conform to a specific body type, believing that happiness and self-worth were contingent upon achieving this *"ideal"* physique. Her experience is shared by countless others, and it was through her own healing process that Megan discovered the transformative power of embracing her body—imperfections and all.

Through years of self-reflection and growth, Megan began to break free from the grip of diet culture and societal beauty ideals. She realized that her value was never tied to the size of her body but to her inherent worth as a human being. This realization became the foundation for her advocacy work. Today, Megan uses her platform to encourage others to let go of perfectionism and embrace the unique, beautiful selves they already are.

Megan's voice on social media, where she has amassed a large following, is one of unapologetic authenticity. She regularly shares personal stories, real-time challenges, and triumphs, all while encouraging her followers to redefine beauty on their own terms. Her body-positive messages are a call to action for women to stop comparing themselves to unrealistic standards and instead, celebrate the things that make them unique. Megan's impact has been felt not only in the realm of body image but also in mental health. Her openness about her struggles with mental health and the importance of self-care has resonated with countless individuals, giving them the permission to care for their mental well-being without shame.

As a mental health advocate, Megan speaks out about the link between body image and mental health, highlighting how deeply interconnected our perceptions of ourselves are with our overall sense of well-being. She is a strong advocate for breaking the silence surrounding mental health issues and prioritizing self-care as a critical aspect of self-love. Megan's platform is not just about promoting body positivity; it's about empowering women to take control of their mental health, free from the toxic pressures of external expectations.

One of Megan's most powerful messages is that confidence comes from within. True beauty is about loving and accepting yourself, flaws and all. It's about recognizing your worth regardless of how society may try to define you. Megan encourages her audience to embrace their bodies with gratitude and compassion rather than focusing on perceived flaws or striving for unattainable standards. Through her posts, she educates and inspires others to break free from the cycle of comparison and embrace the beauty that lies in diversity and individuality.

Megan's influence has sparked an important cultural shift, one in which women are empowered to define beauty on their own terms. Through her advocacy, she's helping to dismantle the harmful notion that beauty is confined to a particular size, shape, or look. Instead, she celebrates the truth that beauty is about self-expression, confidence, and acceptance.

As we explore the themes of beauty, wellness, and style this May, Megan's work reminds us that confidence is not a product to be bought but a mindset to be cultivated. It's a state of being that comes from embracing your true self and caring for your mental health and body in a way that feels right for you. Megan's platform is a space where women are encouraged to make peace with their bodies, prioritize their mental well-being, and step into their power with unapologetic confidence.

Megan Jayne Crabbe's journey from body insecurity to body positivity is an inspiring reminder that beauty is not about fitting a mold; it's about breaking free from it. It's about showing up as your authentic self and embracing the uniqueness that makes you who you are. This May, as we focus on mental health and the importance of self-care, let Megan's message be a guide: love yourself, care for yourself, and radiate confidence from the inside out. Because when you choose to accept yourself, you unlock a beauty that is truly limitless.

FENIX TV

YOUR PLATFORM, YOUR VOICE, YOUR POWER!

Step into the Spotlight as a Host on FENIX TV!

Are you ready to amplify your message, inspire others, and be part of a groundbreaking network dedicated to **empowering women worldwide**? FENIX TV is your platform to **shine as a host**, share your expertise, and connect with a global audience.

WHY HOST ON FENIX TV?

- Reach a worldwide audience passionate about empowerment
- Showcase your voice, brand, and expertise
- Join a community of inspiring leaders and changemakers
- Be part of a network that uplifts and celebrates women

Whether you dream of leading a talk show, sharing powerful stories, or educating and inspiring others—FENIX TV is where your voice matters!

SPOTS ARE LIMITED! Secure your hosting opportunity today.

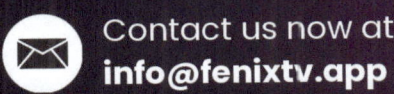 Contact us now at **info@fenixtv.app**

 Learn more at **https://fenixtv.app**

BREAK FREE:

A Heart-Centered Path to Healing Fibromyalgia

By Michelle Seguin

Fibromyalgia is so much more than chronic pain. It's the silent scream of a nervous system pushed to the edge, a body begging to be heard, and a soul quietly asking, *"Can we come back home now?"*

I know this because I lived it. My symptoms began around age 32 after a minor stroke. I was working a high-pressure job, balancing career and family, constantly pouring from an empty cup. What I didn't know then was that my body had been whispering for years. When I didn't listen, it started to scream with pain, brain fog, and exhaustion.

1. Listen to the Body's Cry for Help
Eventually, my body shut down. I spent nearly two years on bed rest. Some days, the pain was so intense I could barely use the remote. I couldn't play on the floor with my granddaughter. She had to climb onto the couch beside me to spend time with me.

I went to countless specialists who told me it was all in my head. Their dismissiveness only caused me more anger and frustration. But the pain was real. It wasn't until my body broke down entirely that I finally heard what it had been trying to say all along: Slow down. Come back to yourself. You're allowed to heal.

2. The Trauma-Fibro Connection
It's easy to focus only on the physical symptoms of fibromyalgia when they're so overwhelming. But once I began working on the trauma, layer by layer, I saw the truth. Fibromyalgia was my body's way of expressing everything I had suppressed for so long.

After losing my beautiful son, Devin, I stopped believing I deserved joy. I carried guilt, grief, and unspoken sorrow. But the moment I gave myself permission to feel again, to process the pain, and to live, things began to shift. I realized my body wasn't betraying me. It was asking for care and attention.

3. Shift from Survival to Safety
The turning point came during the worst flare-up of my life. I was down to eating Jell-O and drinking water, and even that caused unbearable pain. I lay there, curled in the fetal position, tears streaming down my cheeks, and then I felt the choice rise inside me: give up and go be with my son... or fight for my life.

I chose to fight.

That's when the healing began. I used affirmations to calm my mind, meditation to find peace, and somatic tools to reconnect with my body. I did trauma work, met my inner child, and learned what it meant to love myself. It wasn't easy, but it was real, lasting change.

4. Build a Body You Trust
Flare-ups used to send me to the hospital, where I'd be put on morphine for a week. Sometimes, I'd sense one coming and rest, and it would subside. But other times, it still knocked me down no matter what I did. That unpredictability was one of the hardest parts.

What changed everything was learning to understand my body and its signals. Awareness became my anchor. Now, as I release trauma, feel emotions fully, and let them move through me, I truly believe I will never have another flare-up again.

Healing didn't come from a magic pill. It came from choices: peace over pressure, rest over guilt, truth over silence.

Now? I ride horses with my granddaughter, and at 52, I went skydiving for the first time.

So, if you're in the thick of it, please, please listen to your body. It's talking to you for a reason. And when you finally listen? That's when your life begins again.

Connect With Michelle

www.peacefulconnections.ca
www.facebook.com/peacefulconnections

BECOMING
UNDENIABLY U:

Reclaiming Your Identity, Voice, and Power as a Woman in Business

By Valarie Harris

What does it mean to be Undeniably U? It's not just a cute phrase—it's a movement. A mindset. A fierce return to your full, authentic self. The version of you that doesn't apologize for dreaming big, speaking loud, or standing tall in rooms that once tried to shrink you.

And who am I to tell you this?

I'm a woman who climbed the corporate ladder in retail while quietly whispering to herself, *"There's more."* I'm a military brat, a wife, a mom, a marketing strategist, and a freedom-chasing entrepreneur who was never built for a box. I've been told my way of talking wouldn't cut it, my style was *"too much,"* my passion needed to be toned down. I've heard the unspoken *"you're just a woman"* in meetings, interviews and business deals more times than I can count.

But lucky for me, I was raised by two parents who taught me to never let the world define me. They reminded me that I wasn't here to blend in—I was here to stand out.

Undeniably U was born from that truth.

It's for every woman who's been told she's too loud, too bold, too ambitious—or not enough of something else. It's for the women like me who were never told *"no,"* just told, *"do it differently because you're a woman."* Wear this. Say that. Tone it down. Be more likable. Smile more. Don't ruffle feathers.

"You don't need to be more like them. You need to be more like you—bold, brave, and undeniably YOU."

I tried. I tried to follow the mold—until I realized I was suffocating in it.

I had to unlearn the rules written by people who didn't look like me, talk like me, or understand the fire in me. Entrepreneurship was terrifying. Releasing the steady paycheck, the structure, the *"safe path"* wasn't easy. But my spirit craved more. I had stories, skills, and a message that needed to be heard. And I wasn't about to let anyone—especially not my own self-doubt—shut that down.

Being Undeniably U means standing in your truth even when your knees are shaking.
It means building a business (and a life) that reflects your values, your voice, and your vibe.

So to the woman reading this who's scared to speak up, to launch, to pivot, to change—let me say this: You were never *"too much."* You were always meant for more.

Let this be your permission slip to:

Show up without shrinking.
Speak without second-guessing.
Dream without delay.

Because your magic doesn't live in the mold. It lives in your uniqueness. Your lived experiences. Your laughter. Your lessons. Your scars and your sparkle.

I built a brand and a business on being real, raw, and rooted in my truth. I've made mistakes. I've had wins. I've doubted myself. And still, I rise—not in spite of who I am, but because of it.

So the next time someone tells you what *"works"* in business or life, smile. Then go do it your way.

Be Unapologetic.
Be Unrelenting.
Be Undeniably U.

Connect With Valarie

www.VarrisMarketing.com
www.TimeFreedomFreak.com (Not Live Yet, but that's OK to share)
www.facebook.com/varrism
www.instagram.com/coachvalygrlh
www.linkedin.com/in/varrismarketing

GRAB YOUR COPY NOW

WWW.AMAZON.COM/DP/1960136607

She Rises, She Leads, She Lives: Overcoming Obstacles and Thriving Against All Odds brings together Hanna Olivas and 23 remarkable women to share their powerful journeys of resilience, courage, and triumph. From personal loss to societal challenges, each story reveals the strength it takes not just to survive—but to thrive. This inspiring collection is a tribute to the unbreakable spirit of women rising against all odds.

amazon.com   SHOP NOW   SHE RISES STUDIOS

ROCHELLE *BALLARD*:

Empowering Women Through Mindful Beauty and Wellness

In the world of wellness and self-care, there are few who embody the principles of mindfulness, balance, and empowerment quite like Rochelle Ballard. As a wellness entrepreneur and yoga teacher, Rochelle has spent years helping women reconnect with their inner peace, power, and beauty through a holistic approach that integrates mindfulness, yoga, and self-care. Her philosophy is simple yet profound: true beauty begins within, and the key to unlocking it lies in nurturing both mind and body.

May, the season of renewal, is the perfect time to explore ways to refresh our routines and embrace the practices that bring us peace. As we honor Mental Health Awareness Month, Rochelle's approach to self-care is a timely reminder that beauty and well-being are deeply intertwined. It's not just about glowing skin or the latest fashion trends—it's about cultivating a sense of peace and confidence that radiates from the inside out.

Rochelle's journey into wellness and yoga began out of a deep personal need to heal and transform. After years of struggling with the pressures of modern life, including body image issues and stress, she found solace in yoga, mindfulness, and holistic self-care practices. What started as a personal path to healing soon blossomed into a career dedicated to helping others find the same sense of inner peace. Today, she's known for integrating these practices into everyday beauty and self-care routines, guiding women toward a more empowered, centered version of themselves.

One of Rochelle's core beliefs is that beauty is not a product to be applied, but a feeling to be cultivated. By combining yoga with mindfulness, she teaches her clients that true beauty comes from feeling at peace with yourself—body, mind, and soul. When we are centered and balanced internally, that tranquility shines through in everything we do, including how we present ourselves to the world. Her message is clear: self-care isn't a luxury—it's a necessity. And the act of caring for yourself, both physically and mentally, is the ultimate form of self-love.

Through her yoga practice, Rochelle encourages women to slow down, breathe deeply, and listen to their bodies. The modern world moves at a fast pace, and many of us are constantly juggling responsibilities and obligations. In this environment, it's easy to forget that self-care isn't just about pampering yourself occasionally—it's about creating space for yourself every single day. By integrating mindfulness into beauty routines, Rochelle helps women tune in to their needs, understand their desires, and take the time to nurture their physical and emotional well-being.

Her wellness practices extend far beyond the yoga mat. Whether it's through her beauty workshops, her guided meditations, or her self-care rituals, Rochelle teaches women to approach beauty and self-care with intention. She encourages a mindful approach to skincare, advocating for rituals that nourish the skin while calming the mind. She also emphasizes the importance of nourishing the body through clean, whole foods and regular movement, grounding every beauty routine in a foundation of holistic health.

Rochelle's teachings reflect a deep understanding of the connection between mental health and physical well-being. She recognizes that true beauty stems from a harmonious relationship with oneself, and when we take the time to care for our minds, we naturally feel more confident, radiant, and empowered. This connection is at the heart of her work— teaching women to embrace self-compassion and redefine what beauty means in a world that often tries to define it for us.

For Rochelle, mindfulness is the bridge between beauty and wellness. It's a tool that not only calms the mind but also brings awareness to how we move, breathe, and care for ourselves. Whether she's teaching a yoga class or sharing a beauty tip, her emphasis is always on mindful presence. By taking the time to truly be in the moment, we allow ourselves the grace to feel empowered, beautiful, and at peace.

As we celebrate Mental Health Awareness Month and reflect on the importance of self-care, Rochelle's work reminds us that beauty is so much more than skin deep. It's about nurturing the connection between mind, body, and spirit, and honoring the space that exists within us. In a world that often places external beauty above all else, Rochelle's message is a refreshing reminder that confidence, self-love, and inner peace are the foundation of true beauty.

So this May, as we step into a season of renewal, let Rochelle's wisdom be your guide. Take time to breathe, slow down, and honor your body and mind. Through mindful beauty practices, yoga, and intentional self-care, you can unlock a deeper sense of confidence and radiance that comes from within. Because when you feel empowered on the inside, that confidence will naturally shine through, illuminating every aspect of your life.

RECEIVE LIKE A QUEEN, GIVE LIKE A GODDESS:

The Real Secret to Unlimited Abundance

By Dawna Campbell

Let's get real. For so many of us—especially women—receiving can feel awkward as hell. Whether it's compliments, money, help, or recognition, we somehow turn it into guilt, discomfort, or a hundred reasons why we're not quite *"ready"* for it.

But what if I told you this one shift—learning how to receive with intention—could be the very thing that unlocks limitless abundance in your life?

Let me take you back to Japan.

I was shopping for a gift. Not just any gift—something special for a mentor who had deeply impacted my life. I spotted a sake set in a quirky little novelty shop. Cute. Sweet. Affordable.

But something felt off. My friend nudged me and said, *"You should check the department store."*

I'll be honest, I didn't want to. Time was tight. But I went. And there, tucked into a glowing display of elegant ceramics, was a collection of the most stunning sake sets I'd ever seen. Like, jaw-dropping gorgeous. The kind of beauty that made you stop breathing for a second.

And then I looked at the price tag.
Cue panic.

"This is too much," I told myself. *"This is luxury. It's just a gift."*

But my friend looked at me and dropped the wisdom bomb that changed everything:
"It's about where you choose to receive from. If you go where the value is, that means you are open to receiving that value. You have the privilege to receive."

Boom.
It hit me like a cosmic slap across the face.

That was the moment I got it.
Receiving isn't selfish. Receiving isn't shameful. Receiving isn't excess.
Receiving is preparation for sharing. It's how you multiply the blessing.

See, most of us were taught that generosity is about sacrifice. That to give, you must go without. But what if that belief is what's actually blocking abundance.

What if the flow of abundance depends on how well you receive it—and how freely you let it move through you? Let me drop some real talk on you. *"Abundance is not something we hold—it's something we host."* Wealth, love, wisdom, opportunity... they don't belong to us. They move through us.

When you receive with openness and give with generosity, you become a channel instead of a container. And that's where the magic happens.

You ever try to hold water in your hands for too long? It slips through your fingers, right?

When you let it flow—through pipes, rivers, channels—it moves, it spreads, it multiplies. That's what abundance does. It grows when you circulate it. Not when you hoard it. Not when you cling to it in fear. Not when you think, *"If I give this away, there won't be enough left for me."*

That is scarcity talking. That is fear pretending to be wisdom.

So here's the shift:
Next time you receive—whether it's money, support, joy, praise, or divine inspiration—don't stop the flow.

Ask yourself:
How can I let this move through me?
Who else can benefit from what I just received?
How do I turn this moment into a ripple effect?

Because the more you give, the more space you create to receive. The more you receive, the more power you have to give. It's a feedback loop of expansion. And it works every damn time.

So whether it's a luxurious sake set or a sacred piece of wisdom... receive it fully. Not just for you—but for what it will become through you.

Abundance is not meant to stop with you.
It's meant to start with you.

Connect With Dawna

she wins
Women's Network

Empowering Women Entrepreneurs to Thrive Locally and Globally

Transform your life and business with access to exclusive resources, strategic networking, and unwavering support.

Benefits:
- ➤ Strategic networking & mentorship
- ➤ Masterclasses & exclusive resources
- ➤ Member spotlights & VIP perks

Join for just

$87/MONTH

no contracts, cancel anytime.

Start thriving today. Join She Wins Women's Network!

www.shewinswomensnetwork.com

THE *GRIEF* NO ONE TALKS ABOUT:

3 Steps to Healing

By Danica Alison

What do you do with grief that has no funeral, no condolences, no clear goodbye? The kind that lingers in the spaces where someone should be but isn't. The loss of a child you loved but weren't meant to keep. The unraveling of a relationship that faded without closure. The moment you wake up and realize you no longer recognize yourself.

Some losses are obvious. The world acknowledges them and offers support. Others slip through the cracks, leaving you wondering, Does this even count? Am I allowed to grieve this?

I know this grief. I felt it when I lost my marriage, not just the relationship but the version of myself inside it. I felt it when I said goodbye to foster children, knowing they were never mine to keep but loving them as if they were. I felt it when I realized my identity was shifting, unsure of who I was beyond the roles I had always filled.

There is no roadmap for these kinds of losses, but I've learned that there are three steps that can help with healing.

1. Name Your Grief. It's Real

One of the hardest things about ambiguous and disenfranchised grief is that it often goes unrecognized. Without a death certificate or a formal goodbye, it's easy to feel like your pain isn't valid. But grief is not just about death. it's about loss.

Maybe you lost a relationship, but there was no breakup, just distance. Maybe you're mourning a parent who is still alive but emotionally unavailable. Maybe you miss the person you used to be before trauma reshaped you.

Naming your loss gives it weight. It allows you to say, *"This happened. This matters. I am allowed to grieve at this."*

2. Let Go of the Need for Closure

We often hear that *"closure"* is the goal of healing. But when loss is ongoing or unresolved, waiting for closure can keep us stuck.

Ambiguous grief lingers because there's no finality. You may still love someone who is no longer in your life.

You may still feel the pull of an identity that no longer fits. Instead of seeking closure, try to find ways to hold both grief and growth at the same time.

Healing does not mean erasing what was lost. It means learning how to carry it differently.

3. Find Validation. Even If Others Don't Give It

Disenfranchised grief can be isolating because the world often doesn't acknowledge it. Maybe people tell you, It wasn't really your child. You'll find someone else. You should be over it by now. Their words might make you question your own emotions.

But you don't need permission to grieve. The loss of a foster child, a divorce, a friendship that faded, the person you used to be before life changed you—all of it is real. And you deserve support, even if others don't understand.

If no one around you validates your grief, validate yourself. Find spaces where you can process it safely. Talk to those who do understand. Give yourself permission to feel, without apologizing for it.

Healing is Possible

Grief without closure or recognition can feel impossible to navigate. Grief doesn't just go away. It shifts, reshapes, and becomes part of your story. But it doesn't have to define you. Healing isn't about forgetting. It's about learning to carry it in a way that allows you to move forward.

And you don't have to do it alone.

If you're carrying grief that feels invisible, I see you. If you're navigating loss that doesn't fit inside the usual expectations, you are not alone.

Connect With Danica

www.DanicaAlison.com
www.Linktr.ee/DanicaAlison

UNSHAKEABLE:

The Story of a Woman Who Chose to Rise

By Monica Connolly

For many women, life becomes a balancing act of caregiving, career, and responsibilities, often at the expense of their own well-being and dreams. I know this struggle because I lived it.

For years, I was the one everyone relied on—the caregiver, the provider, the one holding everything together. I believed strength meant sacrificing my needs, pushing through exhaustion, and making sure everyone else was okay. It nearly cost me my life.

I'll never forget sitting in a doctor's office, exhausted and in pain, hearing the words that shook me to my core:
"If you don't make drastic changes, you are going to die soon."

At the time, I was battling severe obesity, chronic pain, and a heart condition. But what most people didn't know was that I was also struggling with a binge eating disorder. Food had become my comfort, my escape, and the way I coped with emotions I didn't know how to process.

I didn't even recognize the woman looking back at me. I wasn't just physically sick—I was emotionally and spiritually depleted. I had spent years pouring into everyone else, and there was nothing left for me.

That was my breaking point—but also my turning point.
I made a choice: I wasn't just going to survive—I was going to heal and thrive.

Over the next two years, I lost 150 pounds, but more importantly, I gained myself back. I healed my gut, rewired my mindset, and redefined who I was—not just for me, but for the women I knew were suffering in silence.

Through that transformation, I discovered a powerful truth: women are constantly told to put themselves last. They push through and try to be everything for everyone, and in the process, they lose themselves.

I knew I had to help change that narrative. That's why I became a Certified Holistic Health Coach, Master Life Coach, and Mindset Transformation Expert. My coaching isn't just about weight loss or wellness—it's about helping women reclaim their identity, reset their health, and realign with their purpose.

True transformation happens when we build lives that reflect our values and passions. For many women, that means stepping into entrepreneurship—not just to earn income, but to create businesses that leave a lasting legacy.

Through my Rise & Thrive coaching programs, I help women gain clarity, rebuild confidence, and take empowered action in their health, mindset, and leadership. Whether they're just starting their wellness journey or ready to launch a book, podcast, or business, I provide the accountability, tools, and strategy they need to grow.

That's why I also created:
- **Ember to Empire: A Women's Collective** – A networking and leadership community for ambitious women ready to rise.
- **The Rise & Thrive Mastermind** – A space for launching purpose-driven businesses and stepping into bold visibility.
- **The Unshakeable Belief Podcast** – Where I share real stories and strategies to help women build belief and take action.
- **My Upcoming Book, Made for More** – A guide to help women break free from limitations and embrace transformation.

If there's one thing I want every woman reading this to know, it's this:
You are not stuck. You are not broken. You are ready for more.

I know what it feels like to be exhausted and uncertain. But when a woman decides to take back her power, everything changes.

My mission is to educate, mentor, and empower the next generation of women leaders and changemakers. Because when women rise, families thrive, communities grow, and we build a ripple effect of impact that lasts for generations.

Now let's rise.

Connect With Monica

www.monicaconnollycoaching.com
www.facebook.com/monica.a.connolly.7
www.linkedin.com/in/mnconnolly
www.instagram.com/monicaconnollyandco

MEET *ELISE MORGAN:*

The Powerhouse Behind The Elise Morgan Experience Podcast

Elise Morgan is a former personal trainer, fitness model, professional athlete turned life coach, author, speaker, and healer on a mission to help you reclaim your power and create a life you love. Known for her bold, no-nonsense attitude and infectious energy, Elise brings personal development to life with a twist of sass, humor, and authenticity. Her podcast, The Elise Morgan Experience, is a journey of transformation where no topic is off the table, and every conversation leaves you empowered and ready to take action.

Elise's path to becoming the force she is today wasn't without its struggles. From overcoming toxic relationships and people-pleasing habits to navigating life's toughest challenges, Elise's story is one of resilience and self-discovery. Her own experiences have shaped her approach to coaching and personal development—showing that anyone, no matter what , can unlock their potential and live a life they love.

Elise dives into the real, raw aspects of life with a unique perspective. This podcast is for anyone looking to level up and break free from living a limited life. Whether you're dealing with divorce, grief, PTSD, the loss of loved ones, betrayal, or simply want advice and guidance on having confidence and showing up as the best version of yourself, Elise's podcast is a space to find inspiration, actionable advice, and powerful stories. She talks a lot about the law of attraction, manifesting, and mindset, all of which can help you create the life you deserve.

But Elise isn't alone in this journey. Some of her episodes features exciting guests who bring expertise from a wide range of areas, from personal development and dating to overcoming trauma and finding inner peace. It's a podcast that caters to but not limited to women ,for those ready to make a change and take control of their lives. Elise believes that the key to transformation is a shift in mindset, and she and her guests provide the insights and tools you need to make that shift.

"I believe in the power of the mind ," Elise says. *"Life doesn't have to keep you stuck. We all have the ability to design a life that aligns with who we really are, and that's what this podcast is all about—helping you wake up to the power within you!"*

With each episode, Elise challenges her listeners to take responsibility , bold action and stop waiting for permission to live the life they deserve. Whether it's learning how to set boundaries, heal from past wounds, or cultivate a positive mindset, Elise provides practical advice that's grounded in real-life experiences.

Elise's podcast is a blend of personal development, spirituality, and real talk. It's not just about listening; it's about implementing what you learn into your life , the shifts that will transform how you show up in the world. By weaving her expertise as a life coach with her candid, no-nonsense attitude, Elise helps you navigate the ups and downs of life with clarity, confidence, and grace.

As Elise continues to build her brand, she's creating a space for people to connect, learn, and grow. From one-on-one coaching to workshops and retreats, Elise's goal is to help people tap into their power and create their version of happiness, success, and fulfillment. It's all part of The Elise Morgan Experience, a movement as Elise describes *"to help you live a life you F-In love"*

So, if you're ready to transform your life, break free from self-doubt, and create the future you've always dreamed of, The Elise Morgan Experience is the podcast for you.

THE ELISE MORGAN EXPERIENCE

Connect With Elise

www.instagram.com/theelisemorganexperience
www.youtube.com/@TheEliseMorganExperience
www.podcasts.apple.com/us/podcast/the-elise-morgan-experience-real-talk-on-real-life/id1719459894
elisemorgan@coachelisemorgan.com

TRANSFORMING *STRESS* INTO *SUCCESS:*

The Power of Mindfulness, Fitness, and Nutrition

By Nytisha Davis

In our busy, always-connected world, stress is something many women experience. It can come from being a mother, life partner, employee, caregiver, or simply from being a woman. With so many responsibilities and expectations, it's easy to feel overwhelmed and exhausted. As we go through different stages of life, our bodies and emotions change, adding even more stress. But by focusing on mindfulness, fitness, and nutrition, we can improve our well-being and turn stressful times into opportunities for personal growth.

Recognizing Stress

Stress affects us in many ways, impacting our physical and mental health. It can lead to anxiety, tiredness, and even physical problems. Understanding how stress affects us is the first step toward making positive changes.

I know this from my experience. I became a mother and a wife at young ages 18 and 19. With three kids close in age, I faced a lot of pressure. As a new mom, I struggled with the fear of not knowing how to care for my children and wanting to do everything right. Being a spouse also added its own challenges, as I wanted to be the best partner I could be.

For a long time, I didn't take time for myself. I knew how to love everyone else but often ignored my own needs. It took me years to realize that this constant neglect was affecting my health.

Practicing Mindfulness

Mindfulness means being present in the moment and aware of our thoughts and feelings without judging them. By including mindfulness in our daily lives, we can learn to understand ourselves better, reduce stress, and feel calmer.

Mindfulness can take many forms, like meditation, deep breathing, or simply paying attention to our feelings. For example, when we feel angry or upset, taking a deep breath can help us calm down. I learned to listen to my body and pay attention to how I felt.

As women, we often take on the *"superhero"* role, taking care of everything around us while ignoring our own needs. We need to remember that it's okay to take breaks and care for ourselves too. Doing things like reading a book, going for a walk, hiking, or vacation, or simply kicking your feet up can make a huge difference.

Getting Active: The Importance of Fitness
Physical activity is a great way to relieve stress. Regular exercise not only helps our bodies stay healthy but also releases endorphins, which are chemicals that make us feel good. When we exercise, we feel more energized, confident, and less stressed.

Finding a fitness routine that you enjoy is important. Whether it's running, dancing, yoga, or going to a gym class, the key is to move in a way that makes you happy. Participating in group classes can also create a supportive community, making exercise even more enjoyable.

Having a consistent workout routine helps build discipline and a positive self-image. When we grow stronger physically, we also develop inner strength that changes how we see ourselves.

Nourishing Our Bodies
Food is a critical part of our health and well-being. What we eat influences our mood, energy levels, and even how our skin looks. I found that juicing helped me get essential vitamins more easily while going through the aging process.

After being diagnosed with high blood pressure, I wanted to take control of my health and live without medication. I asked my doctor for advice and began my journey to a healthier lifestyle. I hired a trainer, consulted a nutritionist, and started meal prepping, which was both fun and rewarding.

Mindful eating is about paying attention to how we eat and listening to our bodies. It's important to recognize when we are full and know when to step away from our plates. Staying hydrated is also essential; drinking enough water helps us feel energetic and improves our overall health. Eating fruits and vegetables, like watermelon and cucumbers, can also help us stay hydrated.

Embracing Change
3When we combine mindfulness, fitness, and proper nutrition into our daily routines, we begin a positive transformation. This path leads us away from stress and toward a vibrant, fulfilling life. Mindfulness helps us build awareness, fitness strengthens us, and good nutrition nourishes our bodies.

By embracing these practices, we start to feel more confident and happier. The journey towards reducing stress and experiencing success is achievable, and it can lead to real self-love and empowerment.

As we focus on taking care of ourselves, we also inspire those around us to do the same. By making mindfulness, fitness, and nutrition priorities in our lives, we illuminate our paths and reflect our inner beauty. Ultimately, true radiance comes from within, and by nurturing ourselves, we can embrace our authentic selves and shine brightly in the world.

Connect With Nytisha

wwww.PhillipsMobilelabs.com
www.instagram.com/phillipsmobilelabs
www.facebook.com/phillipsmobilelabs

DANIELLE PEAZER:

Using Fitness to Build Confidence and Achieve Overall Wellness

JADA *SEZER:*

Redefining Beauty, One Bold Step at a Time

In a world that often tries to shrink women into a narrow definition of beauty, Jada Sezer is a voice—and vision—of radical self-love. A model, mental health advocate, and fierce proponent of body positivity, Jada doesn't just challenge the status quo—she transforms it. With every photo, every speech, and every post, she redefines what it means to feel beautiful, confident, and whole.

This May, as we honor Mental Health Awareness Month and explore the empowering theme of Radiate Confidence, there's no better muse than Jada. Her journey is a celebration of both inner and outer radiance—a testament to the power of authenticity, self-worth, and unapologetic visibility.

Jada first made headlines when she ran the London Marathon in her underwear. Yes, underwear. Why? To shatter the myth that only one type of body is *"fit," "athletic,"* or worthy of admiration. The act wasn't a publicity stunt—it was a revolution. Her message was clear: confidence isn't about size; it's about self-belief. Beauty isn't about perfection; it's about presence.

But Jada's story didn't start with a spotlight. Like many women, she spent years grappling with self-doubt, trying to conform to a mold that never quite fit. As a young girl, she didn't see herself reflected in fashion campaigns or magazine covers. She pursued a master's degree in child psychotherapy, deeply interested in the way mental health and body image intertwine. And when she entered the modeling world, it was with a purpose—to shift the narrative, not to fit into it.

Now represented by major modeling agencies and having worked with global brands, Jada uses her platform not just to pose—but to provoke. She invites conversation. She challenges beauty norms. And most importantly, she empowers women to take up space—not just physically, but emotionally, mentally, and creatively.

What makes Jada's voice especially vital in today's beauty culture is her unwavering honesty. She speaks openly about her mental health, the pressure to meet societal expectations, and the ongoing journey of self-acceptance. Her transparency creates a ripple effect—it gives other women permission to love themselves as they are, to ditch comparison, and to redefine beauty on their own terms.

In a season that symbolizes growth and bloom, Jada's presence reminds us that our bodies are not projects—they are homes. And confidence isn't something we find in a mirror—it's something we build, moment by moment, choice by choice. Whether she's gracing the cover of a fashion magazine or speaking on a podcast, Jada's message stays rooted in the same truth: you are enough.

The connection between mental health and body image is real and urgent. The pressure to fit into a filtered world can erode even the strongest sense of self. That's why voices like Jada's matter so much. She doesn't sell an illusion—she offers a mirror, reflecting the strength, softness, and beauty that already exists within each of us.

Jada is also redefining what a model can be. She's not just walking runways—she's walking alongside women, inviting them to rise higher, speak louder, and embrace every curve, scar, and story. Her work bridges fashion and feminism, self-care and activism. And it's that blend that makes her a true icon of this moment.

To radiate confidence isn't about having it all figured out—it's about showing up fully, flaws and all. It's about saying yes to yourself, even when the world says no. Jada's life and career are proof that when women own their worth, they don't just shine—they lead.

This May, as we refresh our routines and refocus on self-love, let Jada Sezer be your reminder: beauty has no size, confidence has no template, and wellness begins with accepting yourself exactly as you are.

So go ahead—wear the bold lip, rock the body-hugging dress, speak your truth, and take up your space. Because when you do, you don't just radiate confidence—you become part of a movement that's changing the world, one empowered woman at a time.

Women's Stories of Strength and Empowerment,
Accompanied by Actionable Strategies on How to Thrive

She GROWS STRONGER

HANNA OLIVAS
Along with 32 inspiring authors

GRAB YOUR COPY NOW

WWW.AMAZON.COM/DP/1960136666

In She Grows Stronger, Hanna Olivas and 31 inspiring authors share powerful stories of women who have transformed adversity into strength. Blending personal journeys with practical strategies, this book empowers readers to rise with confidence and resilience. A compelling guide for growth and self-discovery, it reminds every woman that no matter the challenge, she holds the power to grow stronger.

amazon.com   SHOP NOW   SHE RISES STUDIOS

SHE RISES
S T U D I O S

*U*NLEASH YOUR STORY

BECOME A PUBLISHED AUTHOR!

Have you ever dreamed of sharing your wisdom, experience, or passion with the world? **Now is your time!**

Publishing a book isn't just about writing—it's about **establishing your authority, inspiring others, and creating a lasting legac**y. Plus, with the **$138.5 billion book industry** booming, there's never been a better moment to step into the spotlight.

At **SRS Publishing**, we don't just publish books—we **elevate voices, empower authors, and create change-makers**. Our mission is to help women break barriers, amplify their stories, and thrive in the publishing world. Whether you're an entrepreneur, thought leader, or storyteller at heart, **we're here to guide you every step of the way.**

JOIN THE FASTEST-GROWING PUBLISHING HOUSE FOR WOMEN IN THE USA.

READY TO TURN YOUR DREAM INTO REALITY?

 www.SheRisesStudios.com | *contact@sherisesstudios.com*